Vinaigrette Salad Dressing Recipes

About the Author

Laura Sommers is **The Recipe Lady!**

She is the #1 Best Selling Author of over 80 recipe books.

She is a loving wife and mother who lives on a small farm in Baltimore County, Maryland and has a passion for all things domestic especially when it comes to saving money. She has a profitable eBay business and is a couponing addict. Follow her tips and tricks to learn how to make delicious meals on a budget, save money or to learn the latest life hack!

Visit her Amazon Author Page to see her latest books:

amazon.com/author/laurasommers

Visit the Recipe Lady's blog for even more great recipes and to learn which books are **FREE** for download each week:

http://the-recipe-lady.blogspot.com/

Subscribe to The Recipe Lady blog through Amazon and have recipes and updates sent directly to your Kindle:

The Recipe Lady Blog through Amazon

Laura Sommers is also an Extreme Couponer and Penny Hauler! If you would like to find out how to get things for **FREE** with coupons or how to get things for only a **PENNY**, then visit her couponing blog **Penny Items and Freebies**

http://penny-items-and-freebies.blogspot.com/

© Copyright 2017. Laura Sommers.
All rights reserved.
No part of this book may be reproduced in any form or by any electronic or mechanical means without written permission of the author. All text, illustrations and design are the exclusive property of
Laura Sommers

About the Author ii

Introduction 1

Basic Vinaigrette 2

Mustard Vinaigrette 3

Balsamic Vinaigrette 4

Honey Balsamic Vinaigrette 5

Lemon Vinaigrette 6

Pear Vinaigrette 7

Mussels Vinaigrette 8

No Salt Vinaigrette 9

Smoked Paprika Vinaigrette 10

Dill Vinaigrette 11

Honey Garlic Vinaigrette 12

Basil Vinaigrette 13

Creamy Vinaigrette 14

Caesar Vinaigrette 15

Creamy Balsamic Vinaigrette 16

White Balsamic Vinaigrette 17

Strawberry Vinaigrette 18

Cilantro Lime Vinaigrette 19

Raspberry Vinaigrette 20

Raspberry Balsamic Vinaigrette 21

Spicy Raspberry Balsamic Vinaigrette 22

Honey Dijon Balsamic Vinaigrette 23

Asparagus Vinaigrette 24

Eggplant Vinaigrette	25
Zinfandel Vinaigrette	26
Red Pepper Vinaigrette	27
Orange Vinaigrette	28
Maple-Balsamic Vinaigrette	29
Honey-Lime Vinaigrette	30
Honey Jalapeño Vinaigrette	31
Lemon Dill Vinaigrette	32
Cranberry-Almond Vinaigrette	33
Pomegranate Vinaigrette	34
Pomegranate Molasses Vinaigrette	35
Blueberry Vinaigrette	36
Lemon Anchovy Vinaigrette	37
Sesame-Miso Vinaigrette	38
Cherry Tomato Vinaigrette	39
Toasted Spice Vinaigrette	40
Shallot Vinaigrette	41
Fresh Chive Vinaigrette	42
Olive-Orange Vinaigrette	43
Granny Smith Apple Cider Vinaigrette	44
Creamy Dijon Vinaigrette	45
Mixed Olive Vinaigrette	46
Lemon Tarragon Vinaigrette	47
Whole Grain Mustard Walnut Vinaigrette	48
Citrus Vinaigrette	49
Charred Corn Husk Oil Vinaigrette	50
Lemon Mint Vinaigrette	51

Avocado Lime Vinaigrette 52
Blood Orange Vinaigrette 53
Walnut Vinaigrette 54
Sun-Dried Tomato Vinaigrette 55
Champagne Vinaigrette 56
Warm Bacon Vinaigrette 57
Tabasco Vinaigrette 58
Tex-Mex Vinaigrette 59
Lemon-Soy Vinaigrette 60
Oriental Vinaigrette 61
Peach Vinaigrette 62
Bleu Cheese Vinaigrette 63
Parmesan Vinaigrette 64
Cucumber Herb Vinaigrette 65
About the Author 66
Other books by Laura Sommers 67

Introduction

Bottled salad dressing can be convenient but expensive and they are often full of salt, sugar, and chemical additives. Making your own is simple and allows you to customize the seasonings to suit whatever meal you are preparing.

Vinaigrette salad dressing is light and tasty and comes in many varieties. It isn't just for green salads. Vinaigrette dressing is used on fruit, pasta or even meat.

This cookbook is full of delicious mouth-watering vinaigrette salad dressing recipes for you to try.

Basic Vinaigrette

Ingredients:

1/2 cup red wine vinegar
1/2 cup vegetable oil
1 clove crushed garlic
2 tsps. white sugar
2 tsps. salt

Directions:

1. In a jar with a tight fitting lid, combine vinegar, oil, garlic, sugar, and salt.
2. Shake well.

Mustard Vinaigrette

Ingredients:

1/2 cup white vinegar
1 tbsp. honey
1 tbsp. prepared Dijon-style mustard
1/2 tsp. ground black pepper
2 tsps. salt
2 tsps. minced garlic
1 cup vegetable oil
4 drops hot sauce

Directions:

1. In a small bowl, whisk together the vinegar, honey, mustard, pepper, salt, garlic, oil and hot sauce until thoroughly combined.
2. Chill until serving.

Balsamic Vinaigrette

Ingredients:

1/2 cup extra virgin olive oil
1/2 cup white balsamic vinegar
1 clove crushed garlic
1 tsp. ground mustard
1 pinch salt
Ground black pepper to taste

Directions:

1. In a small bowl, whisk together olive oil, white balsamic vinegar, garlic, and mustard powder.
2. Season to taste with salt and black pepper.
3. Stir in minced fresh herbs if desired.

Honey Balsamic Vinaigrette

Ingredients:

1/2 cup balsamic vinegar
1 small onion, chopped
1 tbsp. soy sauce
3 tbsps. honey
1 tbsp. white sugar
2 cloves garlic, minced
1/2 tsp. crushed red pepper flakes
2/3 cup extra-virgin olive oil

Directions:

1. Place the vinegar, onion, soy sauce, honey, sugar, garlic, and red pepper flakes into a blender.
2. Puree on high, gradually adding the olive oil.
3. Continue pureeing 2 minutes, or until thick.

Lemon Vinaigrette

Ingredients:

1/4 cup olive oil
1 lemon, juiced and zested
1 tbsp. white sugar
1 tsp. Dijon mustard kosher
Salt to taste
Freshly ground black pepper to taste

Directions:

1. Whisk olive oil, lemon juice, lemon zest, sugar, Dijon mustard, kosher salt, and black pepper together in a bowl until creamy and smooth.

Pear Vinaigrette

Ingredients:

1 ripe pear - peeled, cored, and chopped
1/2 cup white wine
1 clove garlic, chopped
2 tsps. Dijon mustard
1/4 cup white balsamic vinegar
1 tsp. ground black pepper
1/4 tsp. sea salt
1/2 cup olive oil

Directions:

1. Blend the pear, white wine, garlic, Dijon mustard, white balsamic vinegar, black pepper, and sea salt in a blender until well combined; drizzle the olive oil into the mixture in a thin, steady stream while continuing to blend.
2. Blend a few seconds longer until the salad dressing is thick and creamy.

Mussels Vinaigrette

Ingredients:

24 fresh mussels, scrubbed and debearded
1 small green bell pepper, seeded and diced
1 small red bell pepper, seeded and diced
1 small yellow bell peppers, seeded and diced
1/2 cup olive oil
1/4 cup red wine vinegar
2 tbsps. chopped fresh parsley
1 hard-cooked egg, chopped
1/2 tsp. salt
1 pinch ground black pepper

Directions:

1. Bring one inch of water to a boil in a large pot.
2. Add mussels, cover, and steam for 3 to 5 minutes, until they are all open.
3. Drain.
4. Remove one side of each shell, and arrange the open shelled mussels on a serving platter. Discard any mussels that do not open.
5. In a medium bowl, mix together the red, yellow, and green bell peppers, olive oil, wine vinegar, parsley, egg, salt, and pepper.
6. Spoon over the mussels on the shells. Refrigerate until serving.

No Salt Vinaigrette

Ingredients:

1/2 cup red wine vinegar
1/3 cup olive oil
1 tsp. lemon juice 2 cloves garlic, crushed
1 tbsp. Italian seasoning
1/8 tsp. white pepper

Directions:

1. Whisk together the red wine vinegar, olive oil, lemon juice, garlic, Italian seasoning, and white pepper in a small bowl.
2. Let stand for at least 15 minutes before serving.

Smoked Paprika Vinaigrette

Ingredients:

1/2 cup red wine vinegar
1/3 cup honey
1 tbsp. stone-ground mustard
1 tbsp. lime juice
3/4 tsp. ground black pepper
3/4 tsp. salt
1 1/4 tsps. smoked paprika
1 clove garlic
2 tbsps. chopped onion
1/4 tsp. oregano
1 pinch white sugar (optional)
1/2 cup olive oil

Directions:

1. Blend the red wine vinegar, honey, mustard, lime juice, pepper, salt, paprika, garlic, onion, oregano, and sugar together in a blender until thoroughly mixed.
2. Drizzle the olive oil into the mixture while blending on low.
3. Chill at least 1 hour before serving.

Dill Vinaigrette

Good on Roasted green beans or cucumber salad.

Ingredients:

1/4 cup vegetable oil
2 tbsps. red wine vinegar
1 1/2 tsps. white sugar
1/2 tsp. dried dill weed
1/8 tsp. salt
1/8 tsp. onion powder
1/8 tsp. garlic powder
1/8 tsp. dry mustard
1/8 tsp. ground black pepper
Add all ingredients to list

Directions:

1. In a blender, combine the oil, vinegar, sugar, dill weed, salt, onion powder, garlic powder, dry mustard and pepper.
2. Blend until smooth, cover and refrigerate until chilled.

Honey Garlic Vinaigrette

Ingredients:

1 cup vegetable oil
1/3 cup apple cider vinegar
3 tbsps. honey
2 cloves garlic, minced

Directions:

1. In a container, combine oil, vinegar, honey, and garlic.
2. Cover, and shake until blended.
3. Set aside for 45 minutes, to allow flavors to combine.
4. Shake again before serving.

Basil Vinaigrette

Directions:

1 cup olive oil
1/3 cup apple cider vinegar
1/4 cup honey
3 tbsps. chopped fresh basil
2 cloves garlic, minced

Directions:

1. In a bowl, whisk together the olive oil, apple cider vinegar, honey, basil, and garlic.
2. Pour over or toss with your favorite salad to serve.

Creamy Vinaigrette

Ingredients:

1/4 cup rice wine vinegar or lemon juice
2 tbsps. Dijon mustard or mayonnaise
1 large garlic clove, minced
Salt and freshly ground black pepper
2/3 cup olive oil

Directions:

1. Measure vinegar (or lemon juice) and mustard (or mayonnaise) into a 2-cup measuring cup.
2. With a small whisk, stir in garlic, a big pinch of salt and a few grinds of pepper.
3. Measure oil in another cup.
4. Slowly whisk oil into mixture, first in droplets, then in a slow, steady stream to make an emulsified vinaigrette.

Caesar Vinaigrette

A smooth alternative to Caesar dressing.

Ingredients:

2 tbsps. white wine vinegar
1 tbsp. Dijon mustard
1 tbsp. balsamic vinegar
1 tsp. lemon zest
1 tsp. white sugar
1/2 tsp. Italian seasoning
1/4 tsp. salt
1/8 tsp. ground black pepper
2/3 cup olive oil
1 clove garlic, minced
1/2 cup freshly shredded Parmesan cheese

Directions:

1. Stir the white wine vinegar, Dijon mustard, balsamic vinegar, lemon zest, sugar, Italian seasoning, salt, and black pepper together in a bowl.
2. Gradually whisk in the olive oil to make an emulsion, or thickened vinaigrette mixture. Stir in the garlic.
3. Add the Parmesan cheese just before serving.

Creamy Balsamic Vinaigrette

Ingredients:

3 tbsps. olive oil
3 tbsps. balsamic vinegar
3 tbsps. mayonnaise
2 tbsps. water
2 cloves garlic, pressed
1 tsp. Dijon mustard
1 tsp. brown sugar
Salt and ground black pepper to taste

Directions:

1. Blend olive oil, balsamic vinegar, mayonnaise, water, garlic, Dijon mustard, and brown sugar together in a blender or in a cup using an immersion blender until smooth.
2. Season with salt and black pepper.

White Balsamic Vinaigrette

Ingredients:

1/2 cup extra-virgin olive oil
1/4 cup white balsamic vinegar
2 tbsps. honey, or to taste
1/2 tsp. sea salt
1/4 tsp. fresh cracked black pepper
1/8 tsp. garlic powder

Directions:

1. Whisk olive oil, balsamic vinegar, honey, salt, cracked black pepper, and garlic powder together in a bowl until smooth.

Strawberry Vinaigrette

Ingredients:

1 cup olive oil
1/2 pint fresh strawberries, halved
2 tbsps. balsamic vinegar
1/2 tsp. salt
1/4 tsp. ground black pepper
1/4 tsp. dried tarragon
1/4 tsp. white sugar

Directions:

1. In a blender or food processor, mix olive oil, strawberries, balsamic vinegar, salt, pepper, tarragon and sugar.
2. Blend until smooth.

Cilantro Lime Vinaigrette

Ingredients:

1/4 cup lime juice
2 tbsps. white vinegar
1/2 bunch cilantro, chopped
1 tbsp. brown sugar
1 clove garlic, minced
1/4 tsp. salt
3/4 tsp. spicy brown mustard
3/4 cup light olive oil

Directions:

1. Blend the lime juice, vinegar, and cilantro together in a blender until smooth.
2. Add the brown sugar, garlic, and salt; blend again until smooth.
3. Spoon the mustard into the mixture.
4. Turn the blender on and slowly pour the olive oil into the dressing mixture in a thin stream; blend until thoroughly combined.

Raspberry Vinaigrette

Ingredients:

1 tbsp. raspberry jam
1/4 cup white vinegar
1/3 cup olive oil
Salt and ground black pepper to taste

Directions:

1. Vigorously whisk together the raspberry jam, vinegar, and olive oil until thoroughly combined.
2. Season with salt and black pepper to serve.

Raspberry Balsamic Vinaigrette

Ingredients:

1/2 cup olive oil
1/4 cup balsamic vinegar
1 tbsp. raspberry preserves
1/2 tsp. onion powder
1/2 tsp. ground black pepper
1/2 tsp. salt

Directions:

1. Whisk together the olive oil, balsamic vinegar, raspberry preserves, onion powder, black pepper, and salt in a small bowl.
2. Continue whisking until thick and smooth.

Spicy Raspberry Balsamic Vinaigrette

Ingredients:

1/2 cup olive oil
1/4 cup balsamic vinegar
1 tbsp. sesame oil
1 tbsp. raspberry preserves
1/2 tsp. salt
1/2 tsp. onion powder
1/2 tsp. ground black pepper
1/4 tsp. cayenne pepper
1/4 tsp. dry mustard

Directions:

1. Whisk olive oil, balsamic vinegar, sesame oil, raspberry preserves, salt, onion powder, black pepper, cayenne pepper, and dry mustard in a bowl until thick and smooth.
2. Cover bowl with plastic wrap; refrigerate at least 1 hour.

Honey Dijon Balsamic Vinaigrette

Ingredients:

1/3 cup balsamic vinegar
1/2 cup olive oil
2 tbsps. Dijon mustard
1 tbsp. honey
Salt and pepper to taste

Directions:

1. Whisk balsamic vinegar, olive oil, mustard, honey, salt, and pepper in a bowl.

Asparagus Vinaigrette

Ingredients:

3 eggs 2 pounds fresh asparagus, trimmed
1/2 cup white wine vinegar
2 tsps. Dijon mustard
1/2 tsp. salt
1/8 tsp. ground black pepper
1/4 cup green bell pepper, chopped
3 tbsps. dill pickle relish 1 tbsp. fresh parsley, chopped
1 tbsp. fresh chives, chopped 1 cup olive oil
8 cups mixed baby greens
4 radishes, sliced 2 tomatoes, quartered

Directions:

1. Place the eggs into a saucepan and fill with water to cover the eggs by 1 inch. Cover the saucepan and bring the water to a boil over high heat.
2. Once the water is boiling, remove from the heat and let the eggs stand in the hot water for 15 minutes.
3. Pour out the hot water, then cool the eggs under cold running water in the sink. Peel once cold and cut into slices; set aside.
4. Meanwhile, place a steamer insert into a saucepan, and fill with water to just below the bottom of the steamer.
5. Cover, and bring the water to a boil over high heat.
6. Add the asparagus, recover, and steam until just tender, 2 to 6 minutes depending on thickness.
7. While the asparagus is steaming, whisk together the vinegar, mustard, salt, pepper, green bell pepper, relish, parsley, and chives in a large mixing bowl.
8. Slowly pour in the olive oil while whisking quickly to create a dressing. Toss the hot, steamed asparagus in the dressing, then place into the refrigerator for at least an hour.
9. To serve, divide the baby greens onto individual plates.
10. Divide the asparagus spears among the salads, then garnish with radish slices, egg slices, and quartered tomatoes.

Eggplant Vinaigrette

Ingredients:

2 pounds small eggplants
1 whole head garlic, peeled and chopped
1 cup olive oil
1/2 cup red wine vinegar
Salt and pepper to taste
1 pinch cayenne pepper, or to taste

Directions:

1. Rinse eggplants, and remove the stems. Place in a large pot of lightly salted water. Bring to a boil, and cook for 10 minutes.
2. Drain, and set aside to cool.
3. In a medium bowl, stir together the garlic, salt, pepper, and cayenne.
4. Cut a slit lengthwise down the center of each eggplant, and pack full of the garlic mixture.
5. Place the eggplants in a glass jar, or glass baking dish. Whisk together the oil and vinegar, and pour over the egg plants to cover. Refrigerate for 2 days before slicing and serving.

Zinfandel Vinaigrette

Ingredients:

3/4 cup extra virgin olive oil
2 oz. sherry wine vinegar
2 tbsps. minced shallot
1 tbsp. chopped fresh parsley
1 tsp. chopped fresh basil
1 clove garlic, minced
Salt and pepper to taste

Directions:

1. Whisk together the olive oil, wine or sherry vinegar, shallot, parsley, basil, garlic, salt and pepper.
2. Allow to refrigerate overnight.
3. Remove from refrigerator and serve at room temperature.

Red Pepper Vinaigrette

Ingredients:

1 red bell pepper, seeded and cubed
1/4 cup balsamic vinegar
1/2 cup olive oil
2 tbsps. honey
1 pinch salt
1 pinch ground black pepper

Directions:

1. Place bell pepper, vinegar, olive oil, honey, salt, and black pepper into a blender.
2. Puree until smooth.

Orange Vinaigrette

Ingredients:

1/4 cup orange juice
2 tbsps. balsamic vinegar
1 tbsp. Dijon-style prepared mustard
2 tsps. honey
1/8 tsp. cracked black pepper

Directions:

1. In a small jar with a tight-fitting cover, combine the orange juice, vinegar, mustard, honey and pepper.
2. Cover and shake well until combined.
3. To store, refrigerate for up to 1 week.
4. Shake well before serving.

Maple-Balsamic Vinaigrette

Ingredients:

1/2 cup balsamic vinegar
1/4 cup maple syrup
2 tsps. Dijon mustard
Salt and pepper to taste
1 cup extra-virgin olive oil

Directions:

1. Place vinegar, maple syrup, Dijon mustard, salt, and pepper into a blender.
2. Pulse to combine, then add the olive oil in a steady stream with the motor running.

Honey-Lime Vinaigrette

Ingredients:

1/4 cup fresh lime juice
2 tbsps. honey
1 tsp. white sugar
1 tsp. Dijon mustard
1/2 tsp. garlic powder
1/2 tsp. kosher salt
1/4 tsp. ground black pepper
1/4 tsp. ground cumin
1/4 cup olive oil
1/4 cup canola oil

Directions:

1. Blend lime juice, honey, sugar, mustard, garlic powder, salt, black pepper, and cumin in a blender.
2. Stream olive oil and canola oil into the juice mixture while blending to emulsify the oil into the juice.

Honey Jalapeño Vinaigrette

Ingredients:

1-1/2 tbsps. - white wine vinegar
1-1/2 tbsps. - fresh lime juice
1 Tbsp. - fresh cilantro, coarsely chopped
1/2 tbsp. jalapeno pepper, coarsely chopped
1 large clove - garlic, quartered
1/2 tsp. - salt
1/4 tsp. - freshly ground black pepper
1/3 cup - honey
1/3 cup - vegetable oil, such as canola

Directions:

1. In a blender, process vinegar, lime juice, cilantro, jalapeno, garlic, salt and pepper.
2. With blender running, add honey, then oil.

Lemon Dill Vinaigrette

Ingredients:

1 tbsp. white wine vinegar
1 tbsp. Dijon mustard
1 tbsp. finely chopped fresh dill
1/4 tsp. finely chopped garlic
1 squeeze lemon juice, or to taste
2 tbsps. extra-virgin olive oil
Salt and freshly ground black pepper to taste

Directions:

1. Stir vinegar and mustard together in a small bowl until smooth.
2. Stir dill, garlic, and lemon juice into the vinegar mixture.
3. Slowly stream olive oil into the mixture while whisking continuously; keep beating until the dressing is creamy and smooth.
4. Season with salt and pepper.

Cranberry-Almond Vinaigrette

Ingredients:

1/2 cup cranberry juice
1 tbsp. lemon juice
1 tbsp. dried cranberries, finely chopped
1 tbsp. finely chopped shallot
1 tbsp. finely chopped fresh parsley
2 tsps. ground almonds
1/2 tsp. crushed red pepper flakes
1/2 tsp. garlic powder
2 tsps. salt
1 tbsp. white sugar
1/3 cup vegetable oil

Directions:

1. Whisk together the cranberry juice, lemon juice, cranberries, shallot, parsley, almonds, red pepper flakes, garlic powder, salt, and sugar in a small bowl until the sugar has dissolved.
2. Whisk in the vegetable oil until the dressing is thick and smooth.

Pomegranate Vinaigrette

Ingredients:

1 cup olive oil
1 cup pomegranate juice
1 cup rice vinegar
1/4 cup white sugar
2 tbsps. chopped shallots
1 1/4 tsps. chopped garlic
1 tsp. ground white pepper
Kosher salt to taste

Directions:

1. Place olive oil, pomegranate juice, rice vinegar, white sugar, shallots, garlic, white pepper, and salt in a blender.
2. Cover and blend until smooth, about 2 minutes.

Pomegranate Molasses Vinaigrette

Ingredients:

3 tbsps. pomegranate molasses
2 tbsps. red wine vinegar
1 tbsp. Dijon mustard
1 tbsp. honey
Kosher salt
Freshly ground black pepper
2/3 cup olive oil

Directions:

1. Whisk pomegranate molasses, vinegar, mustard, and honey in a medium bowl.
2. Season with salt and pepper.
3. Whisking constantly, gradually add oil until emulsified.
4. Season with salt, pepper, and more honey, if desired.

Blueberry Vinaigrette

Ingredients:

3/4 cup vegetable oil
1/2 cup fresh blueberries
2 tbsps. white vinegar
2 tbsps. balsamic vinegar
2 tbsps. honey

Directions:

1. Combine oil, blueberries, white vinegar, balsamic vinegar, and honey together in a food processor.
2. Blend until smooth.

Lemon Anchovy Vinaigrette

Ingredients:

2 lemons
4 anchovy fillets packed in oil, drained, finely chopped
1/2 cup olive oil
1/4 tsp. crushed red pepper flakes
Kosher salt and freshly ground black pepper

Directions:

1. Cut all peel and white pith from lemons; discard.
2. Working over a medium bowl, cut lemons along sides of membranes to release segments into bowl.
3. Squeeze in juice from membranes and discard membranes.
4. Mix in anchovies, oil, and red pepper flakes, breaking up lemon segments against the side of the bowl with a spoon; season with salt and pepper.

Sesame-Miso Vinaigrette

Ingredients:

1 red Fresno chile, with seeds, finely chopped
1/4 cup vegetable oil
2 tbsps. fresh lime juice
2 tbsps. white miso
1 tbsp. reduced-sodium soy sauce
1 tbsp. unseasoned rice vinegar
1 tsp. toasted sesame oil
1 tsp. toasted sesame seeds
1/2 tsp. grated peeled ginger

Directions:

1. Whisk all ingredients in a small bowl.

Cherry Tomato Vinaigrette

Ingredients:

1 pint cherry tomatoes
3 tbsps. olive oil, divided
1 shallot, finely chopped
1 tbsp. (or more) red wine vinegar
Kosher salt, freshly ground pepper
2 tbsps. chopped fresh chives

Directions:

1. Cut half of cherry tomatoes in half. Heat 1 tbsp. oil in a medium saucepan over medium heat.
2. Add shallot and cook, stirring often, until softened, about 4 minutes.
3. Add halved and whole tomatoes and cook, stirring occasionally, until beginning to release juices, 4–6 minutes. Mash some of tomatoes with a spoon.
4. Add 1 tbsp. vinegar and remaining 2 tbsps. oil; season with salt and pepper.
5. Serve warm or room temperature; add chives just before serving.

Toasted Spice Vinaigrette

Ingredients:

1 tsp. coriander seeds
1 tsp. cumin seeds
1 tsp. fennel seeds
1/4 cup olive oil
2 tbsps. white wine vinegar
1 tsp. Dijon mustard
Kosher salt and freshly ground black pepper

Directions:

1. Toast coriander, cumin, and fennel seeds in a dry small skillet over medium heat, tossing, until fragrant, about 3 minutes.
2. Let cool, then chop.
3. Whisk with oil, vinegar, and mustard in a small bowl.
4. Season with salt and pepper.

Shallot Vinaigrette

Ingredients:

1 shallot, finely chopped
2 tbsps. fresh lemon juice
1 tbsp. unseasoned rice vinegar
Kosher salt
Freshly ground black pepper
1/3 cup olive oil

Directions:

1. Combine 1 finely chopped shallot, 2 tbsps. fresh lemon juice, and 1 tbsp. unseasoned rice vinegar in a jar.
2. Season with kosher salt and freshly ground black pepper.
3. Let sit 20 minutes. Add 1/3 cup olive oil and cover. Shake to combine.

Fresh Chive Vinaigrette

Ingredients:

1/2 small garlic clove, finely chopped
Kosher salt
2 tsps. white wine vinegar or fresh lemon juice
2 tbsps. extra-virgin olive oil
1 tbsp. chopped fresh chives
Freshly ground black pepper
8 cups salad greens and fresh herb leaves and tender stems

Directions:

1. Combine garlic and a pinch of salt in a large salad bowl.
2. Mash to a paste with a fork.
3. Mix in vinegar, then oil and chives.
4. Season with salt and pepper. Add greens and herbs and toss to coat.

Olive-Orange Vinaigrette

Ingredients:

1 thinly sliced shallot,
1/8 cup pitted oil-cured black olives, chopped
1/4 cup extra-virgin olive oil
1/4 cup Sherry vinegar
2 tsps. finely grated orange zest
1/4 cup fresh orange juice
1 tsp. coarsely chopped aniseed
Kosher salt to taste

Directions:

1. Mix shallot, olives, olive oil, vinegar, orange zest, orange juice, and aniseed in a small bowl.
2. Season with kosher salt.

Granny Smith Apple Cider Vinaigrette

Ingredients:

1 chopped Granny Smith apple, with peel
1/4 cup apple cider vinegar
1 tbsp. fresh lime juice
1 tbsp. minced shallot
1 tsp. sugar
1/4 cup plus 1 tbsp. safflower or grapeseed oil
Kosher salt to taste
Freshly ground black pepper to taste

Directions:

1. Purée apple, vinegar and lime juice in a blender, occasionally scraping down sides of blender with a spatula, until smooth.
2. Strain mixture through a fine-mesh sieve into a medium bowl, pressing down on solids with spatula to extract all juice.
3. Discard solids.
4. Whisk in shallot and sugar.
5. Whisk in safflower or grapeseed oil until well blended.
6. Season with kosher salt and freshly ground black pepper.
7. Vinaigrette can be made 1 day ahead.
8. Cover and chill.
9. Re-whisk before using.

Creamy Dijon Vinaigrette

Ingredients:

1/4 cup red or white wine vinegar
1 tbsp. Dijon mustard
1 tbsp. honey
1/2 tsp. kosher salt
1/2 garlic clove
1/2 cup vegetable oil, then
2 Tbsp. extra-virgin olive oil
Salt to taste
Freshly ground black pepper to taste

Directions:

1. Pulse vinegar, Dijon mustard, honey, kosher salt, and garlic clove in a blender to combine.
2. With motor running, slowly add vegetable oil, then olive oil.
3. Season to taste with salt and freshly ground black pepper.

Mixed Olive Vinaigrette

Ingredients:

1 small shallot, finely chopped
1/4 cup pitted green olives, crushed
1/4 cup pitted Kalamata olives, crushed
2 tbsps. chopped fresh basil
2 tbsps. olive oil
2 tbsps. red wine vinegar
Kosher salt and freshly ground black pepper

Directions:

1. Whisk shallot, green and Kalamata olives, basil, oil, and vinegar in a medium bowl.
2. Season with salt and pepper.

Lemon Tarragon Vinaigrette

Ingredients:

2 tbsps. fresh lemon juice
2 tbsps. minced shallot
1 tbsp. chopped fresh tarragon
1 tbsp. Dijon mustard
1/2 cup olive oil
Kosher salt, freshly ground pepper

Directions:

1. Combine lemon juice, shallot, tarragon, and Dijon mustard in a small bowl.
2. Gradually whisk in oil. Season to taste with salt and pepper.

Whole Grain Mustard Walnut Vinaigrette

Ingredients:

2 tbsps. Dijon mustard
2 tbsps. whole grain mustard
2 tbsps. Sherry vinegar
1/2 cup olive oil
1/2 cup walnut oil
Kosher salt and freshly ground pepper

Directions:

1. In a medium bowl, whisk together Dijon and whole grain mustards, vinegar, olive oil, and walnut oil; season with salt and pepper.
2. Alternatively, place ingredients in a 1-pint jar with a lid and shake vigorously to combine.
3. Refrigerate until ready to use.

Citrus Vinaigrette

Ingredients:

1 small shallot, finely chopped
3/4 cup olive oil
1/4 cup Champagne vinegar or white wine vinegar
3 tbsps. fresh lemon juice
2 tbsps. fresh orange juice
1/4 tsp. finely grated lemon zest
Kosher salt and freshly ground black pepper

Directions:

1. Combine first 6 ingredients in a small jar.
2. Season vinaigrette to taste with salt and pepper.
3. Shake to blend.
4. Vinaigrette can be made 1 week ahead.
5. Cover and chill.
6. Shake before using.

Charred Corn Husk Oil Vinaigrette

Ingredients:

1 cup vegetable oil
5 oz. firm tofu, drained, cut into pieces
3 tbsp. fresh lemon juice
2 tbsp. apple cider vinegar
1 tbsp. honey
1 ear of corn, in husk
Kosher salt and freshly ground black pepper

Directions:

1. Preheat broiler.
2. Shuck corn, reserving husk; discard silk and set aside corn for another use.
3. Place pieces of husk in a single layer on a broiler proof baking sheet. Broil until charred and blackened in spots, about 4 minutes.
4. Let cool slightly.
5. Purée charred husk and oil in a blender until husk is the size of confetti and oil is darkened in color.
6. Strain mixture through a fine-mesh sieve into a bowl. Makes about 1 cup infused oil.
7. Purée tofu, lemon juice, vinegar, honey, and ¼ cup corn husk oil in a blender until smooth.
8. Season with salt and pepper.
9. Reserve remaining oil for another use.

Lemon Mint Vinaigrette

Great for grilled eggplant.

Ingredients:

1 small garlic clove, finely chopped
1/3 cup extra-virgin olive oil
1/4 cup chopped fresh flat-leaf parsley
1/4 cup chopped fresh mint
3 tbsps. fresh lemon juice
Kosher salt, freshly ground pepper

Directions:

1. Whisk garlic, oil, parsley, mint, and lemon juice in a medium bowl.
2. Season with salt and pepper.

Avocado Lime Vinaigrette

Ingredients:

1 ripe avocado
1/3 cup fresh lime juice (from about 2 1/2 limes)
1 tsp. grated lime zest (from 1 lime)
1 cup lightly packed fresh cilantro
1 jalapeño pepper, seeded and chopped (about 3 tbsps.)
1/2 tsp. ground cumin

Directions:

1. Combine all ingredients and 1/2 cup water in a blender or food processor.
2. Purée until smooth.
3. Add more water, as needed, to reach desired consistency.
4. Refrigerate in an airtight container for up to 3 days.

Blood Orange Vinaigrette

Ingredients:

Juice of 1 Blood Orange about 1/4 cup
Zest of 1 Blood Orange
1/4 Cup Avocado Oil or olive oil
1/4 tsp. Sea Salt
1/8 tsp. Fresh Cracked Pepper
1 tsp. Honey
1/2 tsp. Whole Grain Dijon Mustard
1 Tbsp. Apple Cider Vinegar

Directions:

1. Combine all ingredients.
2. Shake or stir and serve.

Walnut Vinaigrette

Ingredients:

1 cup (4 oz.) walnuts, lightly toasted (see Note)
1 cup water
1/2 cup sherry vinegar
2 tbsps. minced shallots
2 tsps. fine sea salt
1/4 tsp. freshly ground black pepper
1/2 cup olive oil
1/2 cup imported walnut oil

Directions:

1. Place all of the ingredients, except the oils, in a blender and process on high speed.
2. With the machine running, gradually add the olive and walnut oils until the vinaigrette is emulsified, about 1 minute.
3. Refrigerate until ready to serve.

Note: To toast walnuts, place the walnuts in a single layer on a baking sheet. Bake in a preheated 350 degrees F. oven, stirring occasionally, until toasted, 8 to 12 minutes. Cool completely.

Sun-Dried Tomato Vinaigrette

Great for pasta salad.

Ingredients:

1/2 cup sun-dried tomatoes
1/4 cup fresh-squeezed orange juice (about 1 medium orange)
3 tbsps. extra-virgin olive oil
1 tbsp. apple cider vinegar
1/2 tsp. salt
1/4 tsp. freshly ground black pepper

Directions:

1. For the vinaigrette:
2. Place the sun-dried tomatoes in a food processor and pulse to chop.
3. Add the orange juice, olive oil, vinegar, salt and pepper.
4. Process to a slightly chunky, relatively thick puree.
5. Pour over cooked pasta such as fusilli and enjoy!

Champagne Vinaigrette

Ingredients:

1/2 cup extra-virgin olive oil
3 tbsps. Champagne vinegar
1 tsp. honey
1 tsp. Dijon mustard
Kosher salt and freshly ground black pepper

Directions:

1. Combine the olive oil, Champagne vinegar, honey, mustard, 1/2 tsp. salt and a few grinds of pepper in a mason jar and shake vigorously until emulsified.

Warm Bacon Vinaigrette

Ingredients:

4 slices center-cut bacon
2 tbsps. chopped shallots
3 tbsps. red wine vinegar
1 tsp. Dijon mustard
1/4 tsp. freshly ground black pepper
1/8 tsp. sugar
3 tbsps. olive oil

Directions:

1. Heat a medium nonstick skillet over medium heat.
2. Add bacon to pan; cook until crisp.
3. Remove bacon, reserving 1 1/2 tbsps. drippings in the pan.
4. Crumble bacon.
5. Add crumbled bacon and shallots to pan.
6. Cook for 1 minute, stirring frequently.
7. Remove from heat, and stir in vinegar, mustard, pepper and sugar.
8. Gradually add olive oil to the vinegar mixture, stirring constantly with a whisk.

Tabasco Vinaigrette

Great on turnip greens.

Ingredients:

1/4 cup Champagne vinegar
1 tbsp. chopped shallot
1 tsp. fresh lime juice (from 1 lime)
1 tbsp. honey
1 tsp. kosher salt
1 tsp. Dijon mustard
1 tsp. Tabasco sauce
1/2 cup olive oil

Directions:

1. Stir together vinegar, shallot, and lime juice in medium bowl, and let stand 5 minutes.
2. Whisk in honey, salt, Dijon, and hot sauce.
3. Add oil in a slow, steady stream, whisking constantly, until smooth.

Tex-Mex Vinaigrette

Ingredients:

1/2 cup fresh orange juice
1/4 cup fresh lime juice
1 tsp. brown sugar
1/2 tsp. ground cumin
1/2 tsp. salt
1/2 tsp. pepper
1/3 cup olive oil

Directions:

1. Combine first 6 ingredients in a small bowl.
2. Whisk in oil in a slow, steady stream, whisking until smooth.

Lemon-Soy Vinaigrette

Ingredients:

1/4 cup packed light brown sugar
1/4 cup fresh lemon juice
2 tbsps. soy sauce
2 tsps. sesame oil
1/2 tsp. red pepper flakes

Directions:

1. Whisk together brown sugar, lemon juice, soy sauce, sesame oil, and red pepper flakes in a small bowl until combined.

Oriental Vinaigrette

Ingredients:

3 tbsps. honey
2 tbsps. rice wine vinegar
1/4 cup mayonnaise
1 tsp. Dijon mustard
1/8 tsp. sesame oil

Directions:

1. In a small bowl, whisk together the honey, vinegar, mayonnaise, mustard and sesame oil.
2. Pour atop salad and serve.

Peach Vinaigrette

Great on mixed salad greens

Ingredients:

4 medium ripe peaches, peeled
2 tbsp. sugar
2 tbsp. lemon juice
3 tbsp. balsamic vinegar
1/4 tsp salt
1/3 cup vegetable oil
4 cups torn romaine
1 small red onion, halved and thinly sliced
1/2 cup thinly sliced cucumber
6 bacon strips, cooked and crumbled (optional)
1/3 cup chopped pecans, toasted (tossed in butter and brown sugar for a sweeter topping)

Directions:

1. Slice three peaches; set aside.
2. Cut the remaining peach in half; place in a blender.
3. Add the sugar, lemon juice, vinegars and salt.
4. Cover and process until blended.
5. While processing, gradually add oil in a steady stream until emulsified and creamy.

Bleu Cheese Vinaigrette

Ingredients:

4 oz. Bleu cheese
3 tbsp. red wine vinegar
1 c. salad oil
1 1/2 tsp. salt
Dash freshly ground pepper

Directions:

1. Use food processor metal blade, process Bleu cheese for 5 seconds.
2. Add oil, vinegar, salt and pepper to the beaker.
3. Process until well blended. Makes 1 1/3 cups.

Parmesan Vinaigrette

Ingredients:

1/2 cup freshly grated Parmesan cheese
1/2 cup olive oil
2 tsps. lemon zest
3 tbsps. fresh lemon juice
1 tbsp. balsamic vinegar
2 garlic cloves
2 tsps. freshly ground black pepper
1/2 tsp. table salt
1/4 cup chopped fresh basil
1/4 cup chopped fresh cilantro

Directions:

1. Process Parmesan cheese, olive oil, lemon zest, lemon juice, balsamic vinegar, garlic, pepper, and salt in a blender or food processor until smooth.
2. Add basil and cilantro; pulse 5 or 6 times or just until blended.

Cucumber Herb Vinaigrette

Ingredients:

1 small cucumber, peeled, seeded and chopped
1/4 cup extra-virgin olive oil
2 tbsps. red wine vinegar
2 tbsps. chopped fresh chives
2 tbsps. chopped fresh parsley
1 tbsp. plain yogurt
1 tsp. Dijon mustard
1 tsp. prepared horseradish
1 tsp. sugar
1/2 tsp. salt

Directions:

1. Puree cucumber, oil, vinegar, chives, parsley, yogurt, mustard, horseradish, sugar and salt in a blender until smooth.

About the Author

Laura Sommers is **The Recipe Lady!**

She is the #1 Best Selling Author of over 80 recipe books.

She is a loving wife and mother who lives on a small farm in Baltimore County, Maryland and has a passion for all things domestic especially when it comes to saving money. She has a profitable eBay business and is a couponing addict. Follow her tips and tricks to learn how to make delicious meals on a budget, save money or to learn the latest life hack!

Visit her Amazon Author Page to see her latest books:

amazon.com/author/laurasommers

Visit the Recipe Lady's blog for even more great recipes and to learn which books are **FREE** for download each week:

http://the-recipe-lady.blogspot.com/

Subscribe to The Recipe Lady blog through Amazon and have recipes and updates sent directly to your Kindle:

The Recipe Lady Blog through Amazon

Laura Sommers is also an Extreme Couponer and Penny Hauler! If you would like to find out how to get things for **FREE** with coupons or how to get things for only a **PENNY**, then visit her couponing blog **Penny Items and Freebies**

http://penny-items-and-freebies.blogspot.com/

Other books by Laura Sommers

- **Recipes for Chicken Wings**
- **Party Dip Recipes for the Big Game**
- **50 Super Awesome Salsa Recipes!**
- **Easy to Make Party Dip Recipes: Chips and Dips and Salsa and Whips!**
- **Super Summer Barbecue and Pool Party Picnic Salad Recipes!**
- **50 Super Awesome Coleslaw and Potato Salad Recipes**
- **Homemade Salad Dressing Recipes from Scratch!**
- **50 Super Awesome Pasta Salad Recipes!**
- **50 Delicious Homemade Ice Cream Recipes**

May all of your meals be a banquet
with good friends and good food.

Made in the USA
Middletown, DE
20 April 2023

29149451R00042